MORE PRAISE FOR

Ashanti Anderson's refusal and rise ‗‗‗‗‗‗‗‗center me in my communities, and in my Chicananess. because the speakers in *Black Under* are fully aware of the white gaze and are absolutely unconcerned with its survival. Instead, they're focused. Anderson writes, "I erased my smile in another poem because someone said it made no sense," and follows with, "if you want blood I will have for you my red wet grin." I've read these poems again and again, and every time I leave like—*it's we time*. With lines like "throat unbuttons its sound," and "I wish trumpets for my last breath," we end up communing with people who remember themselves, over and over, the way they were, and the way they are and are and are.
—Sara Borjas, author of *Heart Like a Window, Mouth Like a Cliff*

Cutting, saturated, and comprehensive, Ashanti Anderson charts necessary poetry with searing ache. There's so much to unpack here, the painful cacophony white supremacy does to Black spirit, lineage, and innovation yet more profound, the Black dynamism that is beyond erasure. Anderson's debut constructs a world in a concise catastrophe that makes the bones ache. These pages extract traces from graves, from forced stages, from applied pressure of wounds, from more—not to teach, no that's trite, but to gift an anguished aptitude, a surging devastation and love. Language is a beauty in this havoc; "I bow to your darkness like I kneel / besides a child's bed, confessing as gospel ..." Let Anderson guide you there, in that discovery of grief and explanation. In *Black Under*, syllables are catapulted and complicated examinations rife with shape-shifted defiance. Witness Anderson's haunting and marvelous skill.
—Kay Ulanday Barrett, cultural strategist and author of *More Than Organs*, a 2021 Stonewall Honor Award Book

Surprising vernacular, elements of situational discomfort, unexpected and welcome meditations of social impact and situational trauma. There is a subtle and beautiful notion of the absurd within the seemingly mundane of society in general, noted specifically in unreasonable treatment of disadvantaged characters and in the willfulness of perpetrators close and far. These perils leave the audience with a similar, though vicarious, notion and call upon us to do better by ourselves, for others, and with a need to rectify after being delivered into the wrath.
—Allison Adelle Hedge Coke, author of *Look at This Blue*

ASHANTI
ANDERSON

www.blacklawrence.com

Executive Editor: Diane Goettel
Chapbook Editor: Kit Frick
Book and Cover Design: Amy Freels
Cover Art: "Untitled (2020)" by Mariah Quintanilla. Used with permission.

Published 2021 by Black Lawrence Press.
Printed in the United States.

for Azure Iman

CONTENTS

ODE TO BLACK SKIN

You are dark as religion. Remember God
could not have named a modicum of light without you.
You are plum, black currant, passion
fruit in another woman's garden. You are Black
as and as if by magic. Black not as sin, but a cave's jaw
clamped shut by forgiveness. Color of closed wombs and bellies
of ships, you, dark as not the tree trunk but its every cleft.
I chart each crescent moon rising above fingernail
and rub together my thighs for want of you. I try
to find you where the pages of books meet. You hang
where men or piano keys segregate. When I miss you,
I remember the hickey the sun left on the back of my neck.
If I forget, I smoke blunts down to my fingertips
and beg you to come on my lips. This is how I pray for you
when I'm not pessimistic. I bow to your darkness like I kneel
beside a child's bed, confessing as gospel:
There's no monster here.

"I don't want to be at the mercy of my emotions. I want to use them, to enjoy them, and to dominate them."

—Oscar Wilde, *The Picture of Dorian Gray*

CAREER-CHANGING OPPORTUNITY!

Overview:
Make art of the deaths you witnessed. Compensation based on commission. Commitment dependent upon your ability to consistently close sales on open caskets. There is no shortage of this sort of work. May be offered a permanent position.

Job Description:
Curate chalk drawings and teardrops on asphalt. The method: your discretion: mix media, steal life, carve projectiles, engrave shells, etch borders/cross them. For reference, top performers draw blood and conclusions; our most consistent earners chisel anything with jawbone (preference given to candidates using gunpowder and teardrops as mediums).

Responsibilities:
Pose as victim. Expose killer like photo. Make every tear duct a gallery. Exhibit grief.

Qualifications:
- High school degree or equivalent combination of court proceedings, in-school suspensions, and traffic stops
- Ability to lift body out of bed into coffin. May be asked to carry more than one.
- Possess a minimum of five T-shirts, someone else's memory pressed into them
- Willingness to operate unregistered machinery alone as well as in the presence of others
- Unfinished business preferred but not req'd

Benefits:

All employees receive an ID that proves innocence.

Disclaimer: Becomes a gun if you attempt to retrieve it.

Use the company car and credit card! Only
one has been reported stolen.

Click here to apply pressure on the wound.

SELF-PORTRAIT AS OVERSEER

Imagine a ten-year-old with a whip.
In films, it's always a middle-aged man
with a haggard mouth. I also lost teeth, myself
a little snaggletoothed falsetto-swearer.
Movies never show how slaves pissed and shit
themselves, but I've seen surrender embrace
a brother's tense thighs, sheltered nostrils
from the whispered stench of the body's
final prayer.
               The sobbing
not as despairing as his mouth, silent
and open for eons before throat unbuttons
its sound. Leather makes sculpture of skin.
Cotton still lashes my hand, however soft.
I'll give you something to cry for: in photos,
the overseer's clothes never quite fit, hang
over weighted bones like a father's old coat.

BUSTS OF THE BEHEADED

It is rumored that the human brain remains conscious several seconds after being decapitated from the body.

Penny, beheaded after becoming infected with worms from eating soil to supplement her meager rations.

They say sickness come from my back tooth holding mud in its trenches they say me I got worms just make me laugh know nothing live inside me won't be soon to bury itself scooping handfuls of hunger over its own head and even if it grows three seasons it fall one day out my belly and get snatched by traders who say me I don't have time to mother so I beat the names of my nine gone chi'ren in the dirt with this here shovel then I shovel here this dirt with my mouth nurse clay in my jaw 'cause the grits wasn't enough my okra seeds dried up and oysters don't fuck fast as we shuck so I don't believe no worms come inside me they must can see my waggling finger beds to be envy read these dusted lips as want so if a doctor say me I have worms I eat more worms and when they say me going crazy I open wide and say them aaaaaah look here this bubbled mouth ain't a sick it's a cure

Leroy, beheaded for running away to be with his lover.

For you I run past ivy, iron, houndsmaw and high water, find another man's field for where might we twine legs like snakes and bad suggestions. Let us sip skinsalt 'til our lips feel like our bronzed heels and our steel toes have feeling in them again, 'til my breath stinks of daffodil milk, 'til you have followed my constellation of limbs to orison. This spine of mine has never held wicker basket nor whip so it'd be easy for me to think every groan spiritual, every stroke the strike of pickaxe into good ground. I envy the ugly: how gravity nibbles the corners of your lips, unpaid labor tugging on your shoulders each sunrise. I do my best to imitate, bent and open like the shotgun loading, like the half-bitten moon, like misread scripture, like your arched and aching back, the grooves wide enough for my fingertips to ride your river of flesh—

Cane, beheaded for participating in an uprising.

to hold fire in my arms i would give up the whole
length of my neck to only kindle heat with the
curl of my finger you can have my pillowy face
my railroad of spine just so i be able to hail fire
on this plantation and even his children loose
his horses with those tiny fast-moving bits of
light aim at the sky and tear holes into their gods
i would tie my own throat in a bow if only our
oppressors would lick these flames i will let them
bring their own fire to my chest i promise i will
not feel a thing i will already be warmed

SLAVE SHIP HAIBUN

One day a descendant of ours will go on a Carnival cruise and still find time to think of us. She will hear the boom-hiss of a house mix but think *haiwezekani kuwa na amani bila kuelewa*. She will stare down a wave, study its dance moves, note the direction it takes depends solely on the angle of her own glance. And she will wonder: is that the most profound thing she might learn about water.

She will crawl under the bed in an attempt to imagine how we once felt, then curse at having too much space to move. At 6:30 in the morning she will spill a bowl of grits on the liquor-soaked deck and eat the cold, bleached cornmeal with her hands. She will ponder disease. She will envisage death. And she will speculate: the gulls must have stepped near us to pluck between planks for grain as they do now.

But she thinks not of how we watched the birds circle overhead, bomb beak-first into the ocean. Each in our own way, we began to imitate. A few of us induced feathers. I plucked a plume, made a quill.

Crabs scratch backs, claw steel
pail. One's back to another
is a ladder home.

SISTER, PICK WHICH BATTLE TO WIN WHEN YOU CHOOSE TO LOSE THE WAR

I tried staring at the sun once because I needed a metaphor.
I held my head in a lake, breathed sediment,

cut my wrists with tiny blades of sand. I think about suicide
often, I think of other people doing it, I think

about women too strong to be my ancestors
stepping off a ship and into the ocean's font,

that baptism, the salvation of discontinuity. I remember
my heroes shoved their heads inside cannons

to muffle the blow. Their oath: *death is emancipation enforced*
& over & over I repeat I have to tell my baby

THE BODY RECALLS

I'm full of fun
house mirrors.

When my friend
was killed, I turned

to a clock, my arms
wouldn't wind around

any body. Trayvon died
and I was a flag, half-mast

and heavy to lift. For Michael,
I became a pair of shoes, tied,

hanged from a phone line.
For Freddie, a pot. Watch,

I never brought myself
to boil. For Sandra, I

made me a glass,
spilled & cried.

I was already
half-empty.

No more
than ⅗.

LAUGHING TO THE BANK

I don't write of the cartoonish thing split & jagged
at its insides. Instead, how I break even on backs
spindled by hate. I tell God I understand. What
I mean: good people must die to let there be light
in my house. We share a likeness, God and I, both
laughing like green folded our throats. Laugh mean-
while somebody's auntie asks for Anything
Helps. Laugh when people say they don't want to
read about the bad. Crying laughing as we pass
pain off as an offering plate. Sometimes I nervous
chuckle, knowing trauma pays, but the only time
I really laugh is when I'm laughing to the bank.

ACROSTIC FOR MY LAST BREATHS

If I'm ever out of oxygen

Cut the comms. Switch the radio, play
A song by Whitney or Aretha, something
No sense can pause my throat from parting for.
'Gon throw my sorrows into this vast, black void
That don't even have space to hold tune, or blues,

But I don't sing to be heard. I do it to keep on.
Ring diaphragm and rattle lung like sickness, each
Eighth-note a reason to stay living. Can't take
A rest, might hear the sensor's whining,
That worried, heaving falsetto of siren.
How I hate the sound of dying. Rather riff
Even if everything in me stops screaming.

ANSWER TO AN EARNEST PRAYER

True, I don't make mistakes.

But I was trapped
in a man's body
thirty-three years

and I killed myself.

—*God*

CLEANING UP MEN'S MESSES

What of this women's work? It pays unwell, the daily sweep
of bread and glass-crumbs. Grandkids think I'm picky 'cause

I'm always fussing them for even how they walk, sliding feet
scooting my rugs. Just don't want them to notice the cold-

blood stain on the carpet beneath, seeped as I grieved long
before pouring isopropyl alcohol libation. I wipe counters

clean of catsup and remember: glass bottles and hocked spit
lobbed like Molotov cocktails, porcelain plateware broken

across backs of skulls of schoolkids. Built my house with bricks
thrown through my window. When not cleaning commodes

or windows or open wounds, there is much to be sewn, busted
knee needs patching, shirt gnawed by dogs or asphalt, buttons

ran off in another man's fist. Once I'm done with that,
I still got to cook a meal we can all sit down for. Been learned

cold beer move a man much as any fire hose. How I was raised,
women should be felt, not heard. Reverse must be true for men.

If not the ring of a bomb so close it fevers your ear, it's whisky-
thick threats. Every night I hear somebody else's sliding feet

along my neighbor's driveway. Guess they think being strong
means throwing their weight around or starting fires or coming

home to hit women. But men ain't too much different from us.
I too find myself trying hard not to love a man. We all bend

to the will of hard water, know how hard it is to sleep
with a sink full of broken dishes, windows, skulls.

IF

July 10, 1040: Lady Godiva rides through town nude on horseback to force her husband, the Earl of Mercia, to lower taxes.

July 10, 2015: Sandra Bland is pulled over by a state trooper for an alleged traffic violation.

(If) I ride bare-breasted bareback (if my hair were long) trail through a city (if I could convince my husband, if he might contemplate my modesty) to lower injustices (if he were to look) my fuzzy mound to decide be fair (if I could) to the people fair as the under of hand, ride (if I were on a horse) several centuries (if I may) part my river of hair to show the man (if he might stare at my hilly breasts) he think himself an emperor (if I a lady) might he not lower woman like tax (might) bones not beat ground like hooves (if my new clothes were no clothes) (if I stripped and mounted, nude) lesser-ribbed counterpart, (if I undress for him) (if only to change) for every life (if) I want to save (if that includes my own) (if I weren't afraid to) say either of our names (if the officer could have seen her and her mother, too, if) my body brought better, (if) would it mean something that Lady Godiva traversed the city bare (even if many wars ago) hitched hips to horse (as if a lover) the same day Sandra Bland was arrested (if a woman ride a thing might she not be driven beneath it?)?

SELF-PORTRAIT IN BLACKFACE

I am black and black underneath,
my pink lips painted the most
hollerin'est red. Bowtie so tight my throat
yodels, hat stiff as mean lady lips, teeth
crowded and white as my audience.
Hair and shoes both spit-shined,
shit grin wide, belt buckle makes
a fool of sunshine. I look nice
but these folk who pay me pay
no mind.

          These folk clap for any-
thing I say, for they say it's comedy.

One day it'll hit 'em like a punch-
line I'm not a joke. A bit: they give
me top dollar to monologue
their wrongs. But I don't find it funny
as I look, to paint my face the color
of my face just for show-
goers might listen,
                    and they still don't.

IF NO ONE IS AROUND, DOES THIS BODY MAKE A SOUND?

Oh, fluted ribcage, won't you sing
a pretty song, make melody in this
corridor of lung? My chest chimes
like a tongue, diaphragm choirs, &
I wish for trumpets my last breath.

RESIGNATION

This, my too-weak notice. I am tired with comparing my body to heavy things, of holding death like my grandmother's house. I erased my smile in another poem because someone said it made no sense. Understand: I am done writing about the black girl emptied. I'm off to find a brown boy with his ghost still in him. Last week I slipped and busted my mouth on asphalt and if you want the blood I will have for you my red wet grin.

ACKNOWLEDGMENTS

Sincere gratitude to the editors and staffs of the following publications, in which versions of these poems first appeared:

BLAC Imaginarium Zine: "Busts of the Beheaded"

Crab Fat Magazine: "Answer to an Earnest Prayer"

Foothill Journal: "Cleaning Up Men's Messes"

Jet Fuel Review: "Acrostic for My Last Breaths" and "Slave Ship Haibun"

Poetry: "Ode to Black Skin" and "Laughing to the Bank"

Tupelo Quarterly: "Self-Portrait in Blackface," "Self-Portrait as Overseer," and "Resignation"

World Literature Today: "If"

Many thanks to the following programs for providing the time, space, resources, and community that helped bring this book into being: Xavier University of Louisiana, VONA, the Ezra Pound Center for Literature, and UC Riverside's Creative Writing Department (especially BMFA).

Thank you, Black Lawrence Press and Coriolis Company staffs for your care and attention toward my work. And shout-out to Mariah Quintanilla for the amazing cover illustration.

Jasmine Elizabeth Smith, my best friend, thank you for your delicate care for my life and rigorous regard for my work.

LeeLee Jackson, genius! powerhouse! Every word of mine that is read by you is blessed. I am eternally a student of yours.

Nanda Dyssou, I greatly appreciate you for kindly, persistently nudging me toward success, and for championing my work.

Azure, where would I be if not for you? Thank you for always supporting and uplifting me, and for hanging in here with me.

And mostly, Desire', for your attention, patience, reassurance, affection, and [REDACTED], I love you always.

Ashanti Anderson (she/her) is a Black Queer Disabled poet, screenwriter, and playwright. Her debut short poetry collection, *Black Under*, is the winner of the Spring 2020 Black River Chapbook Competition at Black Lawrence Press. Her poems have appeared in *World Literature Today*, *POETRY magazine*, and elsewhere in print and on the web. Learn more about Ashanti's previous & latest shenanigans at ashanticreates.com.